SUNRISE, IN A RABBIT HOLE

Robert Witmer

ISBN: 978-93-6354-847-3

First Edition: 2025
Rs. 200/-

Cyberwit.net
HIG 45 Kaushambi Kunj, Kalindipuram
Allahabad - 211011 (U.P.) India
http://www.cyberwit.net
Tel: +(91) 9415091004
E-mail: info@cyberwit.net

Printed at Repro.

TABLE OF CONTENTS

"Everything tends to make us believe that there exists a certain point of the mind at which life and death, the real and the imagined, past and future, the communicable and the incommunicable, high and low, cease to be perceived as contradictions."
— André Breton

"Nothing returns, nothing repeats, because everything is real."
— Fernando Pessoa, from "When Spring Returns"

"Language [is] chiefly important for the beauty of its sounds, by its possession of words resonant, glorious to the ear, by its capacity, when exquisitely arranged, of suggesting wonderful and indefinable impressions .... the secret of suggestion."
— Arthur Machen, *The Hill of Dreams*

"The whole of life is *nothing* more than questions that have taken unto themselves shape, and bear within themselves the sum of their own answer: and answers that are pregnant with questions."
— Gustav Meyrink, *The Golem*

"Things have one appearance when far away, and quite another when looked at closely."
— Euripides, *Ion*

"Forever bound to ramble free"
— Li Po

And the Gates Shall Not Be Shut by Day

They grow old as they wait
and the ship never passes.
— Pablo Neruda

I expected something more grandiose than this rusty little gate with a broken latch. Maybe not *grandiose*, given the early emphasis on humility, but anyway something more befitting the occasion, more … *revelatory*. But here I am in the altogether, naked as the day I was born, though quite a bit more … developed I should guess, wondering whether to wait for someone to let me in or a great voice calling from on high or maybe just the soft bleating of a lamb, or perhaps I am supposed to continue up the narrow lane to the Big House and announce myself to the man in charge, declaring that I am ready to serve my life sentence. Not *life* exactly, and rather more than a sentence. More like a tome, an opus magnum, something like one of those Victorian novels with their elaborate constructions of minutia and the omniscient narrator who knows everything about everybody, where a poor guy from the sticks gets a job in a factory and, in the end, just has to accept things as they are. I decide to wait, and time passes. And passes. And passes. And, eventually, passes me by.

Hot Date

It just keeps getting hotter. “Out of the frying pan, eh,” I say to her. “Into the fire,” she hisses. “The devil made me do it,” say I. “Snake eyes,” she replies. And so we keep rolling the dice, as we pass the fan magazine back and forth, and dream of celebrity.

moonlight
on marble nipples
the watchman sound asleep

Begin Where You Are

I started walking through walls before I was toilet trained. Not surprisingly, some people took notice, and before the Albanian mafia or TV talent scouts could get their hands on me, a kind old lady in a loose-fitting robe with a tiara took me by the hand and told me I was the vehicle for the return of the Master. Me, me, me. I think I can be forgiven my misunderstanding. A hole in a life through which the sun may pass. I thought being a guru would be fun, and might give me a livelihood. With some savings. A few souls and money to invest. A vintage Lamborghini. Park it anywhere I thought. What are a few tickets for the eyes of the multitude. Disentangled from *māyā* and released from the illusionary nature of things, they would rejoice, and I could party. Or so it seemed. And then. I was arrested for a parking ticket I never paid. Are you kidding me? Six months for blocking the entrance to a pawn shop. But then I thought about it. Yeah, some people need to exchange pieces of their lives for money. Car payments. Rent. That cute little waitress at the donut shop who once asked for correct change. Lives don't change overnight. Spare change. Enough maybe for a cup of coffee, and a donut.

Anchors Away

Shiver me timbers, he would say, apropos of nothing. Shiver me timbers. And a shiver would run down my spine. How could she ever marry such a creep? The guy had a tattoo, a blue anchor on his upper arm, like he had been at Guadalcanal or something – but it was the 2000s, and he was barely out of college. He didn't know a battleship from a bottle cap. Let's play pinochle, he would say, after we finished the beers. I wanted to sweep her off her feet and run away to Florida. Tell her about all those times in grade school when I wrote her name in my notebook. Maybe get a little place near the beach, a fishing boat, make some friends. Who knows. A couple of trips to one of the islands. Find a dealer I could trust. But I knew it was a pipe dream. She was at anchor with her Long John Silver. A safe harbor I suppose. And I was at sea. Swabbing the deck on a Triton submarine.

Fish Out of Water

I went to live in a fishbowl, swimming back and forth, looking out the big window at that strange world I used to call home. A backpack with a survival kit hanging on the coat rack, a cigarette butt in the coffee cup, a news anchor with a hair hat mouthing platitudes on TV while the invisible ventriloquist counted his billions. The other fish didn't have much to say, and I couldn't tell if they were happy. We had to take turns glass surfing because of the overcrowded conditions, and I sensed that my abrupt transformation had adversely affected our shared environment. There was a cute little house at the bottom of the tank, which we had to use one at a time, so I decided to build something bigger, to create a stronger sense of community, when all of a sudden the TV blinked wildly. News was breaking everything in sight. I thought of our little house. And then I realized I had no hands.

Seal of Approval

She fans herself with a trowel she found in the basement of an old house that once belonged to Edgar Allan Poe – or so she says. I can't really trust her, but she pays the bills, and I am just about finished with my novel. A surprise ending, a couple of edits here and there, and then I can go back to the wax museum, where they keep a candle burning in the window. I will be famous then. And once the cement dries, so will she.

Some Things Never Change

I get in line with the seabirds. They seem to be looking at their reflections in the thin film of water behind the retreating wave. So I look down. There I am. In a baggy bathing suit with a snorkel in my left hand. It's hot, and the water smells like gasoline. A kid runs by and the birds scatter. There I am. In a baggy bathing suit – all alone.

a bald tire
on a patch of ice
the world turns

Something

The lion tamer was sad. The tents were coming down and the bearded lady had gone. He went to the cage and whispered something to the sleeping lion, and placed a key in the door. A rich earthy smell followed him out of the encampment and into a dark wood, where he waits.

The Bachelor

I fell asleep. Waiting for the light to change. We were on the third floor, and I was going up. Next thing I know, I'm in the basement, and church bells are ringing. The bride is wearing a floral dress and a motorcycle helmet. The groom is tall. The ring he places on her finger must weigh a ton. She touches her toes and walks out on her hands. The priest waves goodbye. As sunlight pours through the stained glass, a bellboy from a silent film lifts my battered suitcase and starts up the stairs.

Inverted Pyramid

At an advanced age he started writing his magnum opus. A couple of weeks into the thing, he changed his mind. To her mind. The protagonist looked better now, and all her actions were motivated. Nobody took down the shotgun, just to put it back on the wall. The dialogue really worked. Especially as the tension rose with the inevitable conflict. A crisis was approaching. All of his own making. She turned in the doorway. And he died.

winter stars
prayer candles burn
in an empty church

The Grass Is Greener

I met Ponce de León by the fountain of youth. He was full of stories about Mallorca, in the old days, when only a few intrepid travelers were around. Paradise. Here it's all about money. Gold, silver, tobacco, chocolate, the naming rights to popular venues. We wanted a life off the grid, maybe a place in Belize. Forty years later here we are. Problem is, all those intrepid travelers from Mallorca.

a dry martini
civilization
and its discontents

The House on the Hill

Who lived in that house where the lights shone all night and no one came out for the mail? We used to throw stones over the fence, and once, Larry, the crazy one, put a paper bag full of dog poop by the gate. The years flew by and we all grew up and went our separate ways. Still, I can't help but wonder what became of that black cat that used to purr in a funny way as it paced before the door.

Wanderlust

Driven along by an inexplicable desire, the young man follows the crumbs. All one might need, hungering for home. To journey by day. To the end of night. Starlight scribbling old stories across a silent sky. All that passes in darkness. The light beyond light. Fledgling memories. Baby birds. Hungry at home.

leaving the nest
how water flows
through a fisherman's net

I Got That New Retina Screen

I was wondering. What if God made us different colors – blue, red, green, whatever. Some things would have to change. For example, consider the biology of the eye. The cone cells in the eye are sensitive to particular wavelengths of light. Geckos, for example, have excellent color vision at night, making them adept nocturnal hunters. Giant clams observe the world through hundreds of pinhole eyes, sensitive to three different colors of light, yet they are unable to combine the information, though they can detect movement and close their shells. Because of the biological predilection of the human cone cells, we have established particular relationships between words and specific colors. The poet Arthur Rimbaud pointed out the connections between colors and vowels, and the painter Wassily Kandinsky insisted that color affects our emotions. How would we navigate the change from anger to joy and sadness to surprise? Then it dawned on me. These were dangerous thoughts. Start messing with God's plan and before you know it we are transmogrified into traffic signals. Stop. Go. Proceed with caution. Depending on the discretion of the officer. In the end, I suppose, we must live along the limbic pathways of our accorded nature, where vision joins the sunlight and the rain, slowly giving way to a rainbow.

Analogies

I have a theory about the flight of pigeons. The birds often fly back and forth across the ground where I play petanque with friends. Most of the others flinch, some quite dramatically, when a bird suddenly flies by. My view is that the birds are good at flying and prefer not to strike solid objects when doing so, so I don't flinch.

The other day I was walking slowly, very slowly, along the piste when a pigeon flew by in front of me, head high. I was sure the bird knew where it was going so I didn't flinch, nor did I break stride. Then came another, slightly inside the flight path of the first – striking a wing against my head! My theory was challenged and now I am not sure what to think. What if we flew airplanes that way? A jolt in the cabin and the pilot says, "We just hit that building there – with a wing. Sorry."

The point I make above calls into question our tendency to use analogies to the natural world to understand human behavior. Such analogies often fail to fully grasp the situation at hand. Take the irony, apparent in close analysis, of the misleadingly gentle rebuke about crying crocodile tears. While we mean that the person in question is simply feigning deep distress, the analogy suggests a far more horrifying reality. One may reluctantly picture a person having foolishly attempted to cross the croc-infested waters of Cahills Crossing in the Northern Territory of Australia. Distress more red in tooth and claw than any lachrymal dissimulation. Shakespeare had something like the more violent predicament in mind when he wrote that "the mournful crocodile / With sorrow snares relenting passengers."

And what are we really saying when we declare that waves of passion came over him? Against all common sense we imply that only surfers might survive a romantic experience.

Sometimes, however, these human-nature analogies are enlightening. For example, the way we make mountains out of molehills. The Ch'an master famously said that first there is a mountain, and then there is no mountain, and then the mountain is there. To look upon the world from a mole's perspective, with its tremendous power to navigate darkness.

life's calculus
the white chalk squeaks
then the eraser

Oh Lonely Rock

Cold water flutters in the mountain stream beneath the unearthly clarity of a starburst sky. Invisible frogs chirp like happy birds to the pure naked rock wall across the river. The noble passion between a perfect moment and eternity. Doors, windows, words, silent prayer, nor deep meditation could open wide enough to let us in, or out. For the first time I think I understand. A jealous God.

Other Worlds

They meet the fugitive with lamentations.
— Osip Mandelstam

It took forever to get to Mars. All the isolation rehearsals and virtual reality failed to prepare me for what was to come. The others stopped speaking ages ago. We traveled through spacetime like a tin of clams, no longer with any memory of the sea – the trembling plain of Aegir, the girdle of the Earth – pressed together in a slimy silence dreaming of the perfect bouillabaisse. Together with others. Each added one by one, bringing the broth to a boil. Then lowering the heat and simmering in a harmony of flavors. Food for thought. We have arrived. No one moves. There must have been another time. When we thought. We knew. Why. We are here.

Semantics

God is dead, or, strictly speaking, *Gott ist tot*, declared the German philosopher Friedrich Nietzsche. He didn't mean dead like lying in a pool of blood in a dark alley, shell casings circling a rusty drain. No. More like missing in action, or just plain gone – long after the statute of limitations has run out and the paperwork has been filed and the cleverer relatives have found a way to collect on His, or Her, insurance policy. Dog-gone!

Death: To be … lifeless; bereft of sensation or vitality; benumbed; insensible. The bucket kicked; the ghost given up; the dreamless sleep pushing up daisies.

Dead is seldom said. We prefer the deceased, the dear departed, the testator or testatrix. Strange, that there are so many words for beneficiary and just one or two, mostly unknown ones too, for the giver of beneficence. We prefer passing away. Into a realm where tomorrow's dreams awake into yesterday's television programs we can watch on YouTube.

I can't help but wonder. What would YouTube have been called were it a French invention? Would they use the familiar form – such that we would be watching TuTube? Or the formal form – VousTube, which I suppose sounds a bit too much like voodoo?

But we started with God. And God is formless, or so, at least, was the earth when God said *Let there be light*, which, one may presume, He did not do lightly. Or She – but what matter, if God is formless? The light was separated from the darkness, which tells us that God did not create the heavens and the earth at the North Pole in midsummer, though He, or She, might have done, finding it particularly difficult to sleep. That is what too much enlightenment can do.

in failing light
bent over a battered board
checkmate

The Descent

Whenever something goes wrong for me, I feel like someone willed it. Not exactly someone, but rather the One. I know it's just bad luck or coincidence or regression to the mean, but, damn, it feels mean. Unfair. Not partly cloudy, this too will pass, but *Fuck you, buddy, complacent in your happiness.* I'm sure there's a pattern. A squabble on Olympus that triggers the hand of Fate. Words like *inexorable* and *ineluctable* come in mind. I want to strike back. Get even. But more often than not something else goes wrong. I'm not really a pantheist, so I use the Lord's name in vain. Useless I know, but what the Hell? Then I start to wonder: What indeed?

The Question

He opened a can of worms. That old jackknife with the bone handle made a jagged cut, but good enough to get our poles in the water. We were reclining in folding chairs by the lake. *Do you believe in God?* The sun was setting at the far end of the lake, slow ripples sparkling with purples and pinks. The air was still warm. It was quiet. Suddenly a tug on my line. A thump, the pull, the reel speeding into reverse, a struggle for freedom. In less than ten minutes I was holding up a sizeable fish, a rainbow trout. Struggling to remove the hook, I couldn't help seeing that one big eye, staring into my soul, like a bronze Buddha glistening in the rain. *Dinner?* I guess so, I said.

The Return

A rather ordinary butterfly, mostly black with a couple of pale blue spots, lands opposite me on the table in a park where I sit reading. He, she, it – how can you tell – just rests there looking at me. The strange thing is, I know this butterfly, for over the course of three days last summer, at the same table, it came to keep me company. By the third day, I had a weird feeling that this insect knew me and, perhaps, intended to communicate something. I addressed a couple of questions his, her, its way but … nothing, at least as far as I could tell. Then, it disappeared. I thought it must have died, or been eaten by a bird. How long do butterflies live anyway? But that's the question, because the same butterfly is back. I'm sure of it. I am not dreaming, and I sure as hell am not Chuang Tzu. For just a moment last year I wondered whether I was being visited by the spirit of someone I knew. But now …? Suddenly the butterfly wiggles its antennae and flies away. I can't help feeling I'm going somewhere.

Wisdom Is for the Birds

Something tells me a spirit whispers in the ears of the pigeons as they tiptoe over the cherry blossoms, a still small voice telling them they are doves, symbols of purity and innocence. Then I realize that pigeons have no ears, none at least that are visible, though I believe they can hear. Which gets me thinking. What would it be to realize a spirit? Is something real when we believe? How can corn have ears we see when pigeons hide sound behind feathers? What is thinking to our thoughts, and why do we tiptoe round truth, when it is here, in front of our noses? Underground like the roots of the cherry trees. The pigeons coo. And blossoms fall like angels, turning, beautiful, unknowing, each alone.

In-A-Gadda-Da-Vida, Baby

For some reason I read again that essay by Stephen Jay Gould about the ichneumon fly, a study in cruelty if there ever was one, if the notion of cruelty fits the situation, which has been debated for centuries. Gould concludes that we should not look for cruelty or benevolence or any Disney-like moral qualities in nature. Nature is just there, like the ichneumon wasp, hatching away as it eats its victims from the inside out. While the argument that we should not anthropomorphize animals in nature makes good sense, one wonders about the obverse of that perspective: the zoomorphization of human beings. Once upon a time I used to hang out with a guy who brought nothing to the table – a leech, we all thought. But, it turns out that life is like one of those carnival rides where you sit in a teacup and spin around as the entire contraption rotates, spinning and rotating faster and faster until everyone you know has flown off to somewhere else. Scattered to the winds they say. That said, the world is different today. We have Facebook. And the leech is a very successful financial analyst, well-known for his generous donations. Like the Beatles predicted way back in 1969, we have come together. Now effectively marketed amusement parks transport guests into a world of wonder and adventure. With authentic endorsements from influencers building credibility and trust, our parks allow the whole family to enjoy the magic sparkles, the thrills, and the warm fuzzy feeling of nostalgia that real life brings. The spinning teacups rust away behind the boardwalk. Times change.

And yet we remain Kings of the Apes, Lords of the Flies. Although, as our voracious appetites for more increase, we may soon find ourselves eating our home from the inside out, only to discover that the air into which we would fly has become far less amenable to our presence. Kicked out of the

Garden of Eden the first unhappy couple found themselves amongst thorns and thistles sweating out a life of labor until they returned to dust, though not before they conceived a couple of kids. And then, following the first murder, the dissed bro went away from home, heading east, and settled in the Land of Nod. Zoomorphs though we may be, we might not be so lucky, for a nod is as good as a wink to a blind horse. And we have saddled ourselves with the agents of apocalypse. That the kings of the earth must hide themselves in the rocks until the mountains fall.

* The Iron Butterfly song "In-A-Gadda-Da-Vida" is derived from "In the Garden of Eden." Band member Doug Ingle, who wrote the song after consuming a great deal of wine, slurred his words so badly as he sung it for the first time that what was supposed to be "In the Garden of Eden" was interpreted by drummer Ron Bushy, who was writing down the lyrics, as "In-A-Gadda-Da-Vida."

Another Revolution

The fetish wore two masks – tragedy in front and comedy behind. We put him on a potter's wheel and dreamt of civilization, an Earth Sounds LP on the turntable.

Change for a Dollar

Reading about places I travelled in a backpacker's guide from long ago. Rip Van Winkle through a looking glass. When the goodly frames of begone times are no more, what of memories? Tent stakes in lava. The Bishop's hypothetical tree falls in a subliminal forest. Clear cut. The hapless editing of a life story. The face of the land shaved, innocent, inert. Rapacious hands cover the eyes of the blind. Who will not see. Money making the mote in the eye a million dollar mansion. Mountains molehills. Life underground. Dead souls. Remembrances in the mind's eye assume a strange reality. What was is, as it is not. Must be. Zero sum. Summa cum laude. We are poisoning our home.

Cry Uncle

Wolf! the boy cried from somewhere on the hill. Strange, we thought. No one had seen a wolf in these parts for many years. That the boy might be in danger never occurred to us; it was curiosity that led us up the hill. There he was, or they were. Embracing. *My Father!* the boy exclaimed. No one had believed the huntsman. He was not drunk and he didn't look crazy, but a boy living with wolves, who goes into a frenzy at the sight of blood and eats chickens raw. That was just too much to accept. We took the boy in out of pity. There were so many abandoned children in those days, what with the depressed economy, the broken homes, and the endless environmental catastrophes. Eventually the boy began to adjust to life in our village. But now, what were we to do? We offered the wolf a place to stay, not too big, but reasonably comfortable. Not surprisingly, he refused. "I think we'll get it all back one day," he said, as he went away with the boy.

Development

Tree roots are profoundly secretive. What do they get up to down there in the Kingdom of the Dead? Do they dream of green skirts and picnic sheets? Or are they terrified by the prospect of another pig farm? We too have our roots. Way back in time. Sometimes, in my dreams, I hear the lascivious laughter of bonobos screwing their brains out. And sometimes I cover my ears. At the orangutan's heartbreaking cries.

Iðunn, and the Apples of Hel

The roots of dead trees lie exposed to the sun, like snakes in suspended animation. A pretty girl stumbles on the uneven ground, and falls. The boy with a rich father happens by and helps her to her feet, and together they smile. The father is strangely displeased. He has an axe.

The Gardens of Antarctica

August is as free of fissures as a millstone.
— Andre Breton

The gardens of Antarctica breathe free. Free of the hideous white. A dense green silence remembers the blinking ice. Dewdrops heavy as stones hung about the neck. The overpowering poetry of time.

summer
the millstone
grinding
the donkey

The Wisdom of Sex

They sing all day. Shrill music to fill the emptiness their transience assures. Cicadas. Cryptic creatures of the trees. Enchanted with their summery music, they feed on dew and amoretti. So when the gates of dawn are thrown open by a goddess all sweetness and soft beauty, whose insatiable desire has brought her little joy, they pour forth their melodies to the rosy arts of love. And so he succumbs to the gift of a god, and so too must he endure that gift. Tithonus – beautiful, once young, beguiled by the boon of immortality. Aphrodite's curse. The remorseless never-ending curse of time. At the quiet limit of the world. In the beginning is an end, and in the end a beginning. Saltshakers of death. Nymphs underground, waiting to emerge, infected and disemboweled, genitals replaced with fungal spores, now zombies hypersexualized, their unquenchable thirst for love rains down a burden of fluffy seeds, upon their graves, their hidden homes, their future generations. Restored to earth, and there to rise again.

* While underground, baby cicadas (nymphs) may be exposed to the fungus Massospora cicadina, which destroys the insects' genitals, replacing their abdomens with a cavity full of fungal spores, manipulating the bugs into hypersexual behavior to spread the fungus further and transforming the cicadas into what some scientists term "saltshakers of death."

Summer

Few are chosen. Fewer still understand. Tadpoles in a fishbowl resting on a book on evolution. The moment flies by. The quick tongue of the bullfrog. Stabs at the sky.

The Flight of Dreams

I suppose Leonardo flew in his dreams, but I wonder how. His ornithopter was inspired by the flight of winged animals. My own oneiric aerodynamics are more Boeing than bird or bat. There are, of course, no stewardesses or plastic food, and manufacturing flaws don't figure into it, but I never flap my arms, nor is there anything like an awareness of feathered flexion or winged thrust. My airy hopes usually entail take-offs and landings, though they derive from the perspective of a passenger in business class rather than the energetic exertion of a passenger pigeon hopping into the wild blue yonder or, heaven forbid, the crash landing of an albatross. Similar are the aviatory experiences of others I have queried. Descendants of Daedalus though we all are, it seems these slumbery visions of volitation constitute a divorce between our dreams and nature. And thus, dreams, like flora and fauna, may one day become obsolete, something better given over to a virtual reality. One might imagine a Martin Luther King of the future declaiming an "I Have a Conscious State of Hallucinatory Activity Drawn from Darkness" speech, which would have the effect of the original, though without the anaphoric force of the good man's rhetoric. And once again, nothing would really happen. Han Shan wrote his poems on mountainsides. For the wind and the rain and the circling birds of prey. To be here. Dream, parrot poets, of escaping the world. Flap your wings. Dream. The caged bird sings.

Business 101

When I was a kid, I built an ant house. That was before I ever saw one of those ant farm contraptions. I made everything small – the chairs, the tv, the Bible on the end table, even the room where you do number one or number two. After I finished, I showed it to my dad. He kind of laughed and said something about my mom's goofy sister, Aunt Esther. That night, I put my ant house out on the patio. I kept looking through my bedroom window, waiting to see them arrive. First, just one or two, to check the place out. Then more. Until finally the place was on the map. Of course, we couldn't let everyone in. We had to be selective, keep an eye on the bottom line. Reputation, after all, is everything.

Building a Birdhouse

That stuff is for the birds, the builder says, when I point out the loss of shade where the trees would be. He is coming from a power lunch with the architect, a former tightrope walker in his father's circus. Seems like there was a discussion about an extension to the go-kart track. Noise pollution, apparently. What about electric karts, I say, and an aviary just before the final turn? Fat chance, he says. That little hole in front, beneath the red-peaked roof, is too small for the kid's albatross.

Down the Road

I am convinced the dinosaurs knew one day they would be birds. They must have been brimming with confidence and pride. Look at a bird today. Any bird, though emus and chickens are not the best examples. Think birdsong, life on the wing, soaring over the sorrows of sullen earth, wintering in Miami, posing for photographs in the flowering trees. Not now maybe. But one day. An asteroid or two later.

Ringing in the Changes

It might rain. The mighty rain. Kings. CEOs. Just drops in an ocean. Sweet water salted for life. Preserved. Cured. An equalization of solute concentrations. Traced back to antiquity. Survival. Divine retribution. Carcinogen of time. Garum umami, twice blest. It is raining. Pretty hard. The book. Fables for children. Packed with the rest of our gear. Moving to higher ground. Where, in the flooded distance, we see a large covered vessel, an ark of pitched wood. Slowly sinking. In the west. With the whales. Where the light of day dies. Still it rains.

Where the Wind Blows

“Hey, buddy.” I thought I heard the scarecrow call. He was pretty well-dressed. Black hat. Black blazer. A wildflower in his lapel. He seemed to be welcoming me with open arms. “What’s shakin”?” I said. Nothing. I waited for hours. You don’t want to be importunate, even though he started it. Night descended like a murder of crows on our shoulders. A cold wind blew his hat askew. I felt afraid. Suddenly I heard: “Glory to God!” “Who’s that?” “The crows do not fear me. My existence seems pointless. Why am I here, I wondered again and again. But you stopped, and you stayed. And when the wind blew, you were afraid.”

The Accomplice

A blind man moves slowly along the sidewalk, waving his red-tipped cane from side to side. Suddenly he stops and steps toward the street, where a vintage model sports car is parked in a No Parking zone. He collapses his cane like a pirate's spyglass and drops to a knee beside the car. In a flash, the door opens and he gets in. He fiddles with something and the car engine roars to life. I watch him drive away – his loyal dog waiting by the curb.

Mistaken Undertaking

We were drunk when we climbed through the window and saw the coffins. Why not we laughed when we lay down, and fell asleep. The cops didn't think it was funny, guns drawn and pointed at our skulls. "Shoot," you said, wishing under the circumstances to avoid a profanity. Big mistake.

Chuang Tzu

Just one more subscription, that's all I need – the world's last encyclopedia salesman, Willy Loman with an enlarged appendix. It's already pretty dark, and every house has an imposing gate and a vicious dog. Why not just let go. Sit in the shadows and open a volume at random, maybe **G**. Who knows? I might just find myself close to God.

An Odyssey

Here I am on a Greek island 3000 years ago. I have no idea what happened, but there sure are a lot of good-looking ladies here. The problem is they all sound like they're on their way to a fire. Nonetheless they seem to like me. Just yesterday I was Nobody and now I'm Rudolph Valentino. They keep telling me to take the wax out of my ears and relax. My horse came in and I'm set for life. But something's just not right. I've seen this movie before, and I know the best thing to do is to concentrate on my navel and hum. Sometimes it takes a while – but before I know it my clarion call girls are back, insisting that I tell them all about the latest hits.

What Song Can Sing It Back

For years I was captivated by the figure of Cassandra. And once I saw her naked, I lost my mind. She said she was a virgin, but no one would believe her. Then one day it happened. An imminent catastrophe sent stock prices through the roof. Cash in now, my instincts told me, before it is too late. But there was Cassandra, in a silk chiton, reeking of cheap perfume, whispering in my ear: *It's never too late.*

Bowling for Dollars

He was a motorboat racer and she was one of those blonde bombshells that the magician cuts in half. Everything was hunky-dory. But that was before the pandemic. Now she sells bowling shoes door to door and he spends the afternoons texting emojis to a lion tamer in Poughkeepsie. A radio personality somewhere in Texas reckons it was the vaccine, but most people blame the weather. It rained so hard they found mushrooms growing on frogs. Some people, though, insist that it never really happened, that the lion tamer is Ted Turner's yacht and that it is Blondie's half-sister going door to door. All I know is that you just can't trust the sizing on bowling shoes.

I Knew What I Was Doing

She said the kid was hers, from an earlier marriage. But he was six foot three, with a full beard. She was my little sister, and I was almost twenty. Something didn't add up. Besides, I didn't want him in my dorm room, with that pit bull. We decided to cut for it. My sister drew a three of diamonds. The kid got a jack of clubs. I lifted a queen. But the pit bull pulled an ace, of spades. We divided the pot. I got the lawn chair, the helium balloons, and the pellet gun. My sister got the rights to the musical. The kid and the pit bull took the rest. Now, five years later, I'm lost in a forest searching for D. B. Cooper's loot and I run across the kid. He's a junkie. He says the pit bull ran off with some football player. Where's the money?

Play Your Hand

Dave was aggressive, and he always said the wrong thing. Phil always tried to make peace. Billy said nothing at all. One night they were playing poker, when the new guy doubled the bet. “Never played a friendly game, eh asshole,” Dave blustered, as he stared at a straight. “C’mon man. He can bet what he wants,” Phil said, barely glancing at his full house. Billy just lowered his head, his eyes fixed on a royal flush.

Critique of Pure Reason

My way is bound by the rails of reason, but lately I lack the wherewithal for repairs, and there are places where the mountain falls precipitously from the narrow road, at sudden turnings, as it climbs to the next sharp curve, places where the guardrail has fallen away, places I pass in the dark every day, on my way to the fountain of light.

The Old Man's Cadillac

I have the impression the elevator is stuck, though the flashing numbers keep changing, not in the usual order perhaps, but advancing nevertheless. Where am I going? The sky's the limit they say. But the ceiling's as far as the soul of the world can lift me. Floating above the kitchen sink, I watch the dirty dishwater swirl away. To the dark deletive abysm of time.

Bodh Gaya

I suppose I knew. Some bugs eat paint. Having put the finishing touches on a watercolor. I fell asleep.

a beetle
carries a gleam of light
into the roses

The chanting continued. In the temples. And the same stars passed over Siddhārtha. Passed over me.

jewel thief
in the middle of the night
falling stars

Morning awakened. The grass green town. Still. Chanting.

blue flowers
in a tiny garden
the baby's eyes

I rose. The painting on a table. Riddled with spaces. Where eyes and flowers once shone.

innocent bystanders
one by one they drift away
tomorrow's stars

Creative Writing: A Correspondence Course

The failed poet left an epistle for the Mailboxes. Their name was there on the rusty receptacle just inside the crumbling tenement.

To whom it may concern:
Dear Mr. and Mrs. Mailbox,
Yours truly is looking for a post.
I have letters – of reference – a stamp of approval.
I promise to deliver.
RSVP
Yours sincerely,
A Poet Postponed

a ghost
in the machine
writing a wild horse

Days passed. The letters began: To Rearrange Themselves. The Mailboxes came. *Down with their building.* So the rubble rabbled.

swollen eyes
in the damp moonlight
a potato dreams

Once the dust settled and the guilty were booked and the sentences executed, a quiet period followed. He now pursued another line of work – without success.

In the end, nothing happened.

an old song
winks in the waves
madness in the eye of night

Question 1: Identify the literary devices in the prosimetric narrative above.

Question 2: Write a reply to the Poet in iambic pentameter, from the judge's point of view.

Why Writing Is Hard

. . . in the mystery of its own waves
Every earthly voice is shipwrecked.
— Giuseppe Ungaretti

All aboard. The train of Thought. Passing through Words and Ideas on its way to an Ending is leaving a track in the sand. Passengers are requested to refrain from interfering with the duties of the conductor, who may be new to the job, and is having enough trouble keeping his balance, as he squeezes down that narrow aisle, trying to smile, but all the while wishing he was on a boat in the Bahamas.

Begin with the Dictionary

Insipid. Another poem. Gooey batter, tasteless, sticking to the cookie cutter. The frustrated poet texts his agent, for the umpteenth time. Any news? A new voice every hour.

art official intelligence

There's a shop in the strip mall with loads of stuff: Creamsicles, slide rules, first editions. You need to order online. The phone beeps. A classic smiley face upside down. The check is in the mail.

empty street: the scent of her perfume in my earworm

Beyond Good and Evil

The Weiner schnitzel at the joint on the corner is pretty oily, and I think they're using old veal, but it's cheap. I hear Groucho Marx ate there once. Frederick's. Or Fred's, as those of us in the neighborhood call it. Our local piggy bank. Slip a knife through the slot and out comes a quarter, or a dime. It's to put some food on the table. Just call me Karl he said, paid the bill, and he was gone. It was twilight, and the library closed early that night. We had planned it all carefully, down to the minute. Not everything works out though. A day at the races and I'm flat broke. It's hardly a capital offense, and I'm no superman. Some people get lucky. Breakfast at Tiffany's. A night at the opera. If you extrapolate, it's manifest destiny. But I'm still hungry, even though I promised to save you a piece. Not everyone understands philosophy.

Correspondences

Everything is black and white. The patrol car parked by the zebra crossing. The burnt savanna praying for rain. Love the opposite of Law. The angel and the judge. Starlight. In a churning sea. Opposing waves. Hello. Goodbye. The bride has passed away. The groom alone between the sheets. Of music no one sings. The first snowflake on the Eiffel Tower. We rise and fall. The seasons turn. There are so many. Everythings.

Evil Spell

I thought ewe were joking about the guillotine. Sushi for breakfast. A strip stake when the son goes down. Eeny, meeny, miny, moe. Count Dracula and then start looking. And now fare queen my doubt comes dew. Mourning in the roses. Thorns in your crown. A-tisket, a-tasket. My head in a basket.

Fly Paper

If you wish to write a wrong stick to it. A frenzy of wings going seemingly nowhere singing vibrations to pitch perfect ears alive with their worms. Lift that burden you must set down. Your chisel a pen. The hand of a slave. The marble monuments of princes. The principle being for now in the words. Lay your eggs in the dead and rise like the sun. Of man. Of woman. Be as yeast to the windy westerlies in the sale of the century. Canvas the net. Turn right left. Behind. Nothing that is. Must be.

Humpty Dumpty, or Why I Stopped Listening to the Radio

It seems like my thoughts have entered other minds, where they form new imaginations, of things I no longer remember. I used to have ideas. Now they have me. The egg of the world, a vault in space, fertility, dancing with waves, the form of a dove. Hatching new technologies. Golden resurrections from the labyrinth of death. Tut-tut, Akhenaten, tut-tut. The froth on our daydreams is a swan in disguise. The river runs by and you dive in or you build a bridge. Like the internet. Net as bridge. The fly to a spider's belly. The maggot to a fly. Ear pods. Tiny whales sounding. His Master's Voice. Re-mastered and streamed. Now we think together with ourselves. No one's patsy. Stand pat. Blackjack. Nightshade. Our original tongue. Conveyed from the person to the soul of a saint.

Metempsychosis

Of course I can't be sure, but I think I met Houdini in a previous life. He was wiggling out of a straitjacket and I was the straight man in a comedy team coming up next. Half the people in the place were drunk, and most of the others weren't really paying attention. He pulled off the old "Shazam!" and passed us in the wings. "Don't get too close to the bright lights, bozos," he said as he waltzed by. He knew he was on the way up. "Now return," says the Master, and I know it'll be another week before I can reinhabit my past, and give old Harry Houdini a piece of my mind.

Put It on a Postage Stamp

In 1946, the Belgian poet, anarchist, surrealist, and civil servant Louis Scutenaire wrote: “A commendable activity would be the reconstitution of extinct species … It would only take courage, patience and science, and some genius.” 2024. Check. Done, or rather, in progress. Courage. A vexingly subjective judgment. Patience. Well, yes. Sand through the hourglass. Degrees. Experiments. Breakthroughs. Breaking news. Some genius. Determined it was a good thing to do. Big to-do. Making the news, with something old, something new. Nothing new under the sun, saith the Preacher. A game “mixing the rules of chess with those of blindman’s bluff.” A hidden door. Back to the past. The chance of a lifetime. To repeat our mistakes.

Up in Smoke

For my days are consumed like smoke.

A word collector. Every Sunday at dawn. He carries them away in a battered blue van. Just the man who collects them, not those who dispose. However they do. A furnace. A landfill. Each one a snowflake in a winter's tale. The mystery of rime. Hymns like hoar-frost hanging on the trees. The breath of spirits dreams are made on. Puffs of smoke that rise like wisps of larks, whispering to the clouds, twisting to the stars. Blank verse.

> the poet's octopus
> out of ink
> rime on a parking meter

General Store

A morning in winter, the jaundiced sky heavy on the hills, where back in the day they hid from the law, pine needles pricking through snow like an angry porcupine, spring still a far-fetched dream, the pretty girl at the county fair, the kewpie doll from the shooting gallery, wide-eyed kids waiting for fireworks, the big bright purple ones at the end, exploding snowflakes, each unique on the dusty shelves.

Weed wide enough to wrap a fairy in

I watch her weeding. I suppose the flowers like it, not having to share the sun with inferior plants. That afternoon in the museum, as we hurried past the Masaccios to the Masters of the High Renaissance, I followed her like a bloodhound. Iron bars on the windows. Those painted pines in the distance, like green steeples reaching for the light.

The Parson's Tale

Foolproof they said. Fail safe. And then some powdered Pierrot in a cockscomb dressed in motley walks through the door reciting passages from *King Lear*. The jig is up. No further proof needed. We burned the photographs, but the negatives are in a safe in a safe house somewhere out in the sticks. Who knew? CCTV I guess. The eye in the sky. All-seeing providence, like the one-dollar bill. We need not reason our needs. We are cared for by the system. Supply and demand. Caveat emptor. Planned obsolescence. Everything changes. Another place, another time. We were lovers then, and the world was our oyster. We had everything, but you wanted a pearl necklace. The memory of a squirrel. A hollow tree stuffed with nuts no one remembers. Dormant seeds, fruitless relationships, the bellies of baby squirrels. To crawl unburdened to that undiscovered country – unfulfilled. All those paintings Leonardo planned, his flying machine, the Vitruvian Man in a jigsaw puzzle. Trademarked. I remember when the barcode was "no politics, no religion." Scan that. No need to read the fine print. The check's in the mail. And those meddlesome chickens. Here they come. Home to roost.

Politics

I started a fantasy league. We drafted players and the games began. Not everyone was playing the same game however, and conflicts arose, so we changed the rules. But therein, I believe, lay the problem: the attempt at a systematic organization of a blood sport. We aimed at fairness and equity but wound up squabbling about who was in charge and what the powers of authority should be. In an effort to persuade others, the self-interested convinced themselves of their inalienable right to privilege. Flexible modes of thinking gave way to quick ideas, impervious to questioning. Team owners started making trades, regardless whether or not their dealings were evenhanded. From the right hand to the left, under the table. Balanced accounts became zero-sum ledgers. An increasing awareness of mixed-strategy equilibria proved the utility of money in a competitive environment devoid of collaboration or genuine communication with others. What next some of us wondered. One of our more astute participants, a Greek man with a beard, warned that the encroachments of the wealthy were more destructive to the fabric of our constitution than those of players with lesser means. But it was already too late. The community was compromised. What began as an effort to enrich our social lives became an exercise in self-aggrandizement. By the end of the season everyone was bowling alone. Most shops were closed. The bank had moved from the river and some people wanted to reinstate the draft. We had to close the borders. After all, rules are rules.

Il ritorno di Ringo

I keep trying to explain it to Ringo. My dog, a golden retriever. I didn't mean to leave it behind. Not at first anyway. Ringo's willing to fetch whatever it is, but I keep trying to explain. We just can't go there. Private property. The law. The right to bear arms. What's left be damned. The River Styx in your craw, my pet peeve. The apple of discord, my Venus de Milo, retrieved from a poor farmer's field. Her arms around another man. He'll never understand. Ringo. Sniffing the trace of air. The candied root of the sea holly, her aphrodisiac. A golden sun setting in footprints in the sand.

One Afternoon in the Agora

They want to charge me with corrupting the youth. But I'm a fly, I inform them, with a belly full of eggs, baby flies, maggots, the emperor's deathless worms. Eventually they see what I'm buzzing about – my legal defense, an appeal to nature, *lex naturalis*. I don't select my hosts. Their hospitality is a matter of chance, or, perhaps, of certain statistical methods known only to a small cadre of actuaries. An insurance scheme most likely, but definitely above my pay grade. Now, if you will excuse me, there's a young fellow out there somewhere on the front whom I must visit – to lay my burden down.

Sacrificium

Castrato. Can you imagine? I hear that high-pitched voice as my hand trembles over the page. Sharp as steel. How the priests must have fallen over their prayers. And the nuns. Bad habits and all. But the boys, who, as God would have it, would not be boys forever. The enchantments of a perfect soprano, a voice of a flexibility and power no ordinary singer could match. What did they whisper when choir practice ended and the soft light of early spring spilled through the stained glass and Jesus looked almost comfortable on his cross? Did they think about lifting that modest cloth over his loins, stained with the blood of his scourging? Did they cry in a childish way? Music soothes the savage beast, we say. Mistaken though we are. Picture the young shepherd. Blowing his flute. And the wolf. His hunger unsoothed. This is his body. And this his blood. Why am not I at peace? All that beautiful music. *Evviva il coltellino*!

* *Sacrificium* is the title of a recording by opera singer Cecilia Bartoli, which concerns the unsettling history of the castrati. *Evviva il coltellino!* is the Italian phrase enraptured audiences would cry out at performances featuring castrati: Long live the little knife!

Somewhere Over the Rainbow

My wife's cousin is a flat earther. You know, one of those freethinkers who believe that astronauts are actors and Antarctica is somewhere around the edge. You can prove it, apparently, by placing a level on that little tray in an airplane. Anyway, Karl came out of the closet and invited me to one of their conventions. Why not, I thought, and sure enough that round-up brought the mustangs home to roost. One guy had a deep-sea diver's bell on his head, painted like a globe, with crazy eyes at the front. What eyes, or perhaps I's, lay behind that disguise is anyone's guess. Another guy calling himself Kopper Knee Kiss bowed before the Grand Poobah, the Right Honorable District of Columbus, and presented him with a model of the earth that looked something like Ashley Whippet's frisbee. Ironically, among these proponents of homaloidal space were a few rather curvaceous sphere-busters, well-rounded opponents of the Illuminati who disavow the word of God and press their Satanic worldview upon the unwitting masses. These believers all seemed pretty harmless, so it might have been little more than a laugh, except for all that stuff about God and Hitler and Jesuits and Jews. I'm all for a fair dose of skepticism, but the conspiratorial glint in people's eyes and their delusional hyperactivity eventually had me looking for an exit. "Right round the corner," one of the faithful directed me, with a wink. I couldn't help but think about the pure-hearted ones who closed the Globe, and were more or less in favor of burning all theatres to the ground. As one of the flat earth spokesmen had said, "There are things we know: Fire burns."

Target

Some places have done a pretty good job removing the homeless and beggars so you can go shopping with the kids without feeling like maybe you should dig in your pocket for some spare change. Seeing is believing, some say. What you see is what you get, others proclaim. The car is at the far end of the parking lot, a long way from the corral for the shopping carts. It's hot, and the kids are fighting over one of the toys. I don't work here, you reason, and anyway, people need jobs. It's not like it used to be.

Tweezers

As if you cared to remove the flea from its tiny circus. The hair from the tip of your nose. The soul from a fertilized egg. The iron ore must be freed from the mountain. The forge stoked. Clear plastic set to the package so nobody buys the wrong kind by mistake. Not everything, I suppose, is where it should be. Some things need be removed. The tweezers from their little pouch in that vanity case you found at the flea market. That enduring though tiny and dim-getting-dimmer memory from the formidable fabrications of life.

Alchemists

Alchemists. That's what Kyler's friend Tucker calls them. He has a signal, so he's online. *Turning one thing into another. No wonder the country is going to pot.* Something about stoned philosophers who lead a better life in their golden years. *We need to steal ourselves to avoid a similar fate*, Kyler says, or maybe it is Tucker, because he has the smartphone.

The Wrath of Achilles

Go to the ant and be strong.

Fingernails appear to grow on the dead, looking to some like life after death. It is, rather, the deliberate process of death, the wasting of the flesh around the nail plate. Kamikaze pilots cut their fingernails before their missions, sending the clipped nails to their mothers for remembrance, and the family tomb. I ponder these fingernail facts as I clip mine on a park bench, and watch an ant carry one away. The nail sways above the ant like a spar on Charon's boat. What the ants back home will do with my nail I know not. Perhaps it could serve as an arch to enlarge the anthill. Or perhaps these Myrmidons have their own Dr. Frankenstein, who would do one great thing: create a being to fortify the commonality, providing help in modifying habitats, tapping resources, and defending the colony against their enemies. A Prometheus of the emmets, a fallen angel desiring utopia in life beneath the soil. Harmony underground. Until the muffled drums of war sound and the plain is repopulated with warriors, locked in the mandibles of loyalty, fierce and bristling for battle. Everything now is more beautiful, for we are doomed. The sun sets behind the trees. That once underfoot is underground. Like us, ants bury their dead.

Beloved, My Belated, Beloved

I figured it out. Death is a calibrated average of life's boredoms. Nothing much changes, and it goes on forever. What of heaven and hell? One day, out of the blue, an angel turns up with a message: *They have seen the light. Your name is now a song.*

Breath and Shadow

One day, if I'm lucky, strange turn of phrase, I'll be one hundred years old, like the woman before me, seated in the park, where cherry blossoms are blowing under blue sky, the limbs turning green, and I'll laugh at the pictures my nurse snaps on her phone, and pull myself to my feet without her assistance, and laugh again when I stumble, but step ahead on my own, back to the future no one can see.

each wave
another rainbow
my bucket of sand

Carpe Diem

I used to have long hair. Long ago. To belong. A long way from here. I took along a camera. But no longer. Old photographs long for the past, making it harder, I believe, to say: *So long*.

Don’t Look a Gift Horse in the Mouth

A tall guy in a long black coat, looking something like Abe Lincoln at a funeral, except for the funny hood, turned up at my bus stop the other day. There were a lot of people in line, so I gave my place to an elderly lady, who sort of smiled at me as if to say *Thanks a lot*. As the bus pulled away with the tall guy up by the driver, I walked leisurely to the library to return my long overdue copy of Emily Dickinson’s *Collected Poems*, humming a tune by The Grateful Dead.

death’s door
the knocker askew
another eye in the peephole

Eternity

Emily Dickinson. There are so many things we will never understand. Imagine a young woman in a pinafore, with a penchant for prolepsis. An independent spirit who dwelled in possibility, selecting the society of reticence and obscurity, assenting to a divine madness, a poet of uncommon sense, who let the bankers count the nickels and the dimes. She was willing to inebriate the darkness with endless summer days, dazed by the blues, until a stumbling buzz snatched syllables from her sound and she arrived at winter in her room, alone, with zero at the bone. Let the landscape listen to her truth's superb surprise: breathless shadows glisten when stone is turned to snow. And then perhaps to know of the Dane's princely puzzle, the undiscovered country from whose bourn no one returns. Memento mori. Omega. Past the slumbering wonder of near death experiences with their sensations of levitation and total serenity. Doom's electric moccasin. The absolute dissolution of nothingness lets nothing go. The chill, the stupor, the kneeling emperor with agent orange in his hair. Quartz butterflies all: papillon, farfalle, schmetterling, mariposa. The soul singing fifoldara. Farewell. To see what is new with eyes of the dead. From worm to silky chrysalis. Imago. Winged angel in her perfect form. Solemn in her soul. Her secret keeps. Dash not through life but make each pause a whelp of words. This world is not conclusion, though deaf and dumb. The bell's tongue is a swan's song. A funeral in the brain. The evil that lives after us. Les mouches. Time flies. Finnegan's wake. Night's watch. The little folded hands of sleep. The alarm on the Doomsday Clock. Just in time. The pale coachman stops. Kindly for me. And then the wheels turn, a journey's just begun. And when —

Metaphysics

I know I am going to regret this but I want to say something about death. Not death in general, but my own death. That event of utmost uncertainty. The luck that got me here presumably peters out, drops the ball as it were, folds, takes one for the team and determines by way of virtually indisputable statistical evidence to give up the ghost. Yeah. I guess. But some people guess wrong. Guess who. Not the band, though remembrance is a link. Think of a chain: the way one link fits with another. And the way they fit car tires in the snow. When it looks almost impossible to get there, you're rolling again. An occasional slip and a slide but you get there. The low fence the color of snow, the crosses, the wrought iron gate, the others holding black umbrellas, whispering things you shouldn't say aloud. Past the whispers, on the snow, the wheels scrunch to a stop. This time you're really here. Or am I? That's the problem. Whose who?

Sleeping It Off

It wasn't easy. Playing dead. The director was drunk and the enemy soldiers kept breaking ranks. How many times did I close my eyes and try to think of nothing? Again. And again. Something was always wrong. I needed the job, so I didn't complain. And eventually, I fell asleep. When I woke up, some bearded men were playing nine-pins, and drinking wine. It had to be getting late, but the sun was coming up. I tried to stand, but someone shouted *Duck and cover*, so I fell back into my role. You know what déjà-vu is like. Well, this was way weirder. I was still playing dead, but the movie was different. This one seemed almost real. I began to think I was dreaming about the wine. That's all I remember. Now the doctor is telling me it happened a long time ago, and it is true. The war was everything.

Bumbling Along with Beelzebub

He had the answer to everything. It put him in Jeopardy. Classical Pitfalls. What in hell is *terza rima*? Pasta al Dante. The square root of *nein*. Light my fire by the Doors. He never had a chance with Beatrice. Down to his last obol. Live and learn was the lesson. Burn baby burn was the way.

Prisms of Silence

When he didn’t respond, she cast down her eyes. The colors of sunset were threading through copper trees. A leaf blowing away. The empty nests of hungry birds. A squirrel’s nut forgotten in an aging oak. What remains in the end. A question.

Mothers

A crow perches nonchalantly on a neighbor's TV antenna, keeping an eye on the clothesline. Suddenly she swoops into the yard, snatches a baby blue washcloth in her black beak, and flies away. The nest is ready now: clothes hangers covered with straw and odds and ends of appropriated laundry. The blue eggs well-protected. Schoolchildren passing through the park duck away from the frenzied cause. She remembers. The couple wending their way through the Walmart, filling the cart with diapers, pjs, cute little washcloths, a rattle, and, though he kind of objects, a pacifier. They pay and he looks closely at the credit card before tucking it into his wallet and taking her hand. It was the washcloth she used for the baby's first bath, and she cries. It must have been that mean kid next door who took it, but she knows there is no point in asking. When her son gets home from school he has a nasty cut on his head. He says something about a crazy bird, but she suspects another fight with the brat next door. When will it stop? Like the alimony payments. And those damned crows with their god-awful cries.

August

I was Zorro on the carport roof. I always liked black. The handle of my toy gun was black, with a long silver-colored barrel. Kenny was calling from our fort in the sandbox. The summer sky was a deep blue, the backyard all green grass. Up on the roof a warm breeze blew. One tiny cloud, slowly disappearing. Kenny kept calling: *They're coming!*

beneath a frosted apple tree
she cries
the medal on the mantelpiece

The Problem with Zippers

She wants a Scotch Terrier, to lead along the esplanade. I want another shot of Glenlivet, no ice. We can't see eye to eye. She in her designer shades, and mine blurry. Words between us like flurries of snow, in the headlights, of an oncoming truck, in the middle of the road, in the middle of our lives, going on, regardless.

social media
train tracks
arriving at a conclusion

Chiaroscuro

I dropped the bouquet in the first bin I passed. OK. I was wrong. But I said I was sorry. Some people talk to their plants. You sing to yours. A little off-key, but lovely nevertheless. Cut flowers are grown in greenhouses. Sunshine through glass. Water from a moldy hose. Affections arranged in a fluted vase. A harmony of words on a tiny card. Sundown withdraws like a shadow to a corner of the room. The infinite mysteries of life in the dark. Our common atonement. To be. At one with a soul in heaven. A corpse at home in the ground. Draw the curtain and die. Chiaroscuro. We go our separate ways.

Doorstep

She has been gone for more than a week. Walking back from work, I take a shortcut through the park. Her cat, who comes and goes as she pleases, follows me home. At the door, she purrs and rubs against my leg. It's late.

cold milk
in a cracked bowl
moonlight through the doorway

East of Eden

An empty wine bottle. A solitary rose. I glide across the kitchen floor with a glass of water. Let us drink together, you and I. You with your bright red lips and thirsty thorns. Me with what I believe you desire. A failing light darts through the torn curtain. A rickety chair at your feet. There, where I suffer your long narrow neck. Cut from the garden. Where we lived before time.

Glass Houses

I thought an aquarium would be a good idea. Rainbows moving back and forth before the picture window. Sprinkling in a little fish food and watching them purse their lips as if to kiss. What a way to spend the rest of my life. I didn't know she had a traumatic experience in college with "Prufrock," that passage about the sea-girls at the end. They think we're fish, she would say whenever we went to Benny's. I never really thought that much about how angelfish inhabit a similar life space to the handcuffed crabs at Benny's Baltimore Buffet. Anyway, I watch them – well, it's really other them now (the tropical species don't last long) – gliding through the failing light. The postman looking sadly through the window as he takes another letter.

Is This Love

"Last chance," he says, "and I blew it." "There will be other opportunities," she says, "Let it go." "It's gone," he says, as the sun sinks below the horizon and a pink glow flushes the clouds, while, out of nowhere, a chill breeze stirs the curtains through the open window. The kid next door cranks up the volume on an old Bob Marley album, as his mother revs the engine on her motorcycle and drives off. "When will it end?" she wonders. The Earth spinning like a Wailers' LP, the needle making its melodious way to the hole in the center.

Persona non grata

I asked my wife to read an early draft of my novel. The next day she berated me for my first-person narrator. It's a persona I say. No way she says he is you. So you're saying I am I. You are I she says. That got me thinking. I had learned from Walt Whitman that I contain multitudes, and Martin Buber taught me I am thou. But my spouse's assertion of a Gordian Knot of identities had me longing for a sword. I slipped my manuscript into a drawer and went back to work as a ventriloquist. But the narrator from my discarded novel never left my side. He followed me everywhere. And sometimes he pleaded in a soft voice: Let me go home.

Postcards

I listened with impatience to a language I couldn't understand. They ate food I didn't like, and things smelled funny. I preferred to stay home and watch TV, but my parents made me go. I suppose that now the farm is a housing development, similar to where I grew up. Over time, everything became more and more like me – and, slowly but surely, I wished it were different.

That's Amore

Old photos show me my mother was quite good-looking as a young woman. She served in the Women's Army Corps during World War II, driving trucks and helping to guard German and Italian POWs. She told me once that the German prisoners were very stoic, stern-faced and mostly incommunicative, while the Italians were different, chatty, some even amorous. As it turned out, her favorite singer was Dean Martin. However, one must always be wary of stereotypes and all forms of comparison. When the moon hits your eye like a big pizza pie, you may very well be suffering from a cataract. The beautiful winged boy carrying the bow and arrows is sometimes painted blind.

boy and girl
under a single umbrella
not a cloud in the sky

winter blossoms
the elderly couple shiver
together in the shower

lost love
the silence
of a frozen waterfall

The Passionate Shepherd

I finally found a shepherd who agreed to appear in a poem of mine on YouTube. It was to be bucolic, with flute music. I wasn't so sure about the sheep. A bleating lamb or two, maybe, but I had to keep costs down. Do you know what an iambic pentameter goes for these days? No love scene. Just the lament of a lonely soul, a rustic in the rusty light of early evening, longing for love. I had a problem, though. My shepherd was over eighty. I thought it best to avoid any accusations of ageism. But I replaced the flute with a cello. Those deep resonant tones brought a somber gravitas to the scene. Joseph carrying a lamb over blank verse.

Waiting for the Moving of Water

"I could tell by the sound of your footsteps," she says in a kindly voice, before cashing a personal check drawn on a bank in another state. "Trust," she says, sitting in a tiny room behind the barred window, my next meal in her hands. A middle-aged woman in a go-nowhere job, probably dangerous too. "No two people have the same way of walking," she says. "Everyone moves to a different rhythm." I lean forward to take the twenty dollars from her spotted hand stretching through the opening beneath the bars. Just beyond her wistful smile, in a corner of the dingy cubicle, I see the wheelchair.

Walking the Dog

I think I finally understand. Dog walking etiquette, I mean. Wan-wan-chan probably wants it from Chibi-chan, but the lady on the leash is in control. Yap, yap. And then we say hello. Cute dog. You too. Wan-wan-chan is straining against the leash at an increasingly higher pitch, and Chibi-chan is yap-yapping like mad, so we smile our farewells and turn away. Our revels now are ended, and slowly I walk toward home, so too, I suppose, does she, recalling that we just giggled at our dogs' mutual infatuation. I don't know. She probably never read Freud or that bestseller by Xavier Hollander. Man's best friend, they say. But that is nothing more than sexist language, a colonization of canine camaraderie by linguistic manipulation. Dog eat dog, they say. And I think I understand.

Reflection

Who knows? she said, and we left it at that. Years later I wanted to know. It took a while but eventually I realized she was right. A face in the mirror who keeps asking who you are.

Duck and Cover

The Cuban Missile Crisis. I was in grade school and we had drills. The same loud alarm as a fire drill, but a different experience altogether. Instead of walking single file out to the playground, joking around with your friends, we had to sit against a wall in a dark corridor hugging our knees to our hearts. Dead silence was expected. But sometimes we whispered. Kid stuff.

spring rain
children holding umbrellas
upside down

Mushrooms

When the river freezes, the deep fish sleep, drunk beneath the looking glass. Young Alice, searching sage advice, in a field of rosemary, watches summer fade and crouching yellow leaves scrabble the blue whispers of the mushroom's diamond sky. On tiptoes, unrepentant butterflies scent the eucalyptus edges of her mind. Mind you, the walk to Lumle ends the evening dream, and grave tears freeze each snowflake in the breeze.

Step lightly on the stones, young Alice. White rabbits pilot airplanes headed south, and diffidence beguiles the caterpillar. Find that tree in Kodaikanal. Yggdrasil in ashes, the sacred hanging tree, shivering like a fish tail slipping free. Chainsaws for the honeybee.

Toadstool, fungus, Manhattan's cloud. An island for a sail of beads. The beaver's tail owes little to its pelt, banished to vanish on the Susquehanna. Felt hats before the reckoning of silk. Reality will not relent. Her roots die underground, where a parliament of worms weaves each future's tapestry.

Play lutes of light when morning comes, young Alice. There is no one to hear and how. Sand castles sinking with the stars; dolphins moonwalk whale song. The rabbit in a wizard's hat waits for spring, and her green eyes smile back.

Benares

What to make of memories of death. Twice gone. And yet the light in the temple by the holy river and the dirge of the harmonium go on. Antyesti: The body burned in final sacrifice. Go to the waters the scriptures say. Cold ashes fall into the holy river, where they flow away to the sea, the gold in the teeth caught in an untouchable's wicker basket. What remains. Untouched. By death. Or music's memories. Of light at night. A river of dead stars shining overhead. Even life when one was young. Was old. The gods made the river. We made it holy. With our music, our ashes, and our memories.

I am deeply grateful to my good friend Morgan M. X. Schulz for providing invaluable feedback on the pieces in this book.

The cover design was created by my son, Alexander Witmer.

Robert Witmer lives in Tokyo, Japan, where he has resided since 1978. He has published poems and works of prose in many print and online journals. His first two books, *Finding a Way* and *Serendipity*, are available at Amazon and other online booksellers, as well as from the publisher, Cyberwit.com.

www.ingramcontent.com/pod-product-compliance
Ingram Content Group UK Ltd.
Pitfield, Milton Keynes, MK11 3LW, UK
UKHW041315190726
13845UKWH00025B/275